T0161398

THE CAPTAIN'S TIGER

THE CAPTAIN'S TIGER

A Memoir for the Stage

ATHOL FUGARD

THEATRE COMMUNICATIONS GROUP

Library of Congress Cataloging-in-Publication Data

Fugard, Athol.
The captain's tiger : a memoir for the stage / by Athol Fugard. —1st ed.
p. cm.
ISBN 1-55936-164-6 (pbk. : alk. paper)
1. Dramatists, South African—20th century Drama. 2. Voyages around
the world Drama. 3. Young men—Journeys Drama. 4. Seafaring life
Drama. 5. Red Sea Region Drama. 6. Ocean travel Drama.
I. Title
IN PROCESS PR9369.3.F78 C
822—dc21   99-13259
CIP

Cover/Book design and composition by Lisa Govan
Cover Photo by T. Charles Erickson

THE CAPTAIN'S TIGER

The Captain's Tiger: A Memoir for the Stage received its American premiere at the McCarter Theatre Center for the Performing Arts in Princeton, New Jersey, Emily Mann Artistic Director, on May 5, 1998. Stage and costume design was by Susan Hilferty, lights were by Dennis Parichy, sound and original music was by Lulu van der Walt. Susan Hilferty and Athol Fugard were the directors. The cast was as follows:

THE AUTHOR/TIGER	Athol Fugard
DONKEYMAN	Owen Sejake
BETTY	Jennifer Steyn

In January 1999, the above production was then produced at New York City's Manhattan Theatre Club, Lynne Meadow, Artistic Director; Barry Grove, Executive Producer. Darron L. West was the sound designer. The New York cast was as follows:

THE AUTHOR/TIGER	Athol Fugard
DONKEYMAN	Tony Todd
BETTY	Felicity Jones

CHARACTERS

THE AUTHOR

THE TIGER
The Author as a young man

DONKEYMAN
A Swahili crew member of the SS *Graigaur*

BETTY
A photograph of his mother as a young girl

Author's note:
The role of The Author/The Tiger
must be played by the same actor.

SCENE I

The stage. A ship's bell. The Author enters and strikes it eight times.

AUTHOR *(To the audience)*: Eight bells. End of the watch. Imagine you're at the wheel of an old cargo ship steaming slowly across the Pacific. Its the deadman's watch, midnight to four A.M., so the wheelhouse is dimly lit. In front of you is the illuminated face of the compass. You glance at it from time to time to check your course but mostly you're just staring out into the darkness, watching the proud forward mast sweeping the stars as she rolls gently from side to side. Its a calm, clear night with a slight swell so an easy swing of the wheel is all that's needed to keep hold your course. The sailor who is going to take over from you as helmsman is there at your side. You give him the compass bearing and he repeats it to make sure there is no mistake. You greet the officers and then head down to the galley for a mug of strong, hot tea, and because it's that sort of night, you'll sit out on deck, on one of the bollards maybe, and drink your tea and think your thoughts while the ship sails steadily on, the bows lifting and falling in a rhythm as seductive as those hips that gave you such a good time in the last port.

That is how I remember some of my nights on board the SS *Graigaur*. "Graigaur" . . . it's a Welsh word. It means "rock of gold," though by the time I joined her in 1952 she was starting to look more like a rock of rust.

One of the old tramp steamers, any cargo anywhere. A true wanderer of the seas.

My first sight of her was in Port Sudan harbor where she was taking on a cargo of salt for Japan. I knew absolutely nothing about ships so I thought she looked very impressive as I stood there on the quay side, watching the harbor crane dump avalanches of gleaming white crystals into her holds. In any case you can't get to know a lady like her when she's tied up with heavy mooring ropes in a stagnant harbor basin with hordes of shore workers crawling all over her. You need to be out on the open sea for that.

I got my chance a few days later when the last mooring rope was cast off and the tugs started to pull her away from her berth, swing her around and guide her toward the opening in the breakwater. The image that came to me then as I stood there on deck and which still seems so right to me, was of some ancient, blind leviathan, deep rumblings coming from her belly, as she nosed around clumsily looking for her escape, and when she found it, when she slipped past the breakwater and her bows dipped into the freedom of the open sea, I felt a thrill shiver through her rusty old hulk.

The voyage had begun.

I was twenty years old.

SCENE 2

Number Four hatch of the SS Graigaur; *a small folding card table, box to sit on, stack of paper, fountain pen and ink. The Tiger writes a letter to his mother.*

TIGER:

SS *Graigaur*
Somewhere in the Red Sea
August 17th, 1952

Dear Mom,
I sincerely hope you didn't faint when you read the address at the top of this letter. It is not a joke. I am writing to you now aboard the steamship *Graigaur* which is headed for Japan.

Just when I thought my only hope of getting out of Port Sudan was to stow away on one of the ships headed for England, I met Captain Hersee in the bar of the Red Sea Hotel. We started talking and when he heard about my predicament he offered to take me on board his ship as a supernumerary. That means I get a shilling a month, a comfortable bunk in the sick bay and three whopping good meals a day in return for which I have to look after the captain—clean his cabin, make his bed, do his washing, serve him his food . . . a sort of glorified servant. Tell Dad that in sailors' jargon I am what is known as the Captain's Tiger. I think we are going to get on very well. I've only been on the ship a couple of days so I don't really know yet about the rest of the gang. The officers are white and the sailors a real bag of liquorice-all-sorts . . . black, brown and yellow.

But the important news, Mom, is that apart from seeing the world, this is my chance to keep the promise I made you, and settle down at last to serious writing. I'm ready for it now. No more short stories and poems—I'm going for the big one, a novel à la Tolstoy, and its going to be about a beautiful young Afrikaner girl in a white dress in a small Karoo town. Recognize her? That's right! Its the photograph of you when you were a young girl that's hanging in your bedroom. That is going to be my inspiration. I'm going to weave together all the stories you've told me about your life and what you wanted to do with it, only this time all those dreams you had are going to come true. When I finish this letter—I'm writing it on deck outside the sick bay, it's as hot as hell, Mom—I'm going to settle down to my first session.

I'll be posting this letter in Aden. After that the next port of call is Colombo, the capital city of Ceylon. Tell Dad to get a map, a red pencil and a ruler, and to draw straight lines joining up all the places I mention in my letters. That way he can follow me on all my travels and adventures. It will give him something to do. How is he, by the way?

So there, Mom. First Africa, now the world! The great adventure continues.

Your ever-loving son,
The Captains Tiger

(*Folds his letter and puts it in an envelope which he addresses. After that he prepares, with great deliberation, for his first session of writing . . . filling the fountain pen, organizing the paper, moving his chair to a different side of the table etc., etc. While he is doing all this, Donkeyman appears on deck. He is a big, fierce-featured, black man, bare-chested and wearing short trousers and sandals, his body gleaming with sweat. He has just come up from the engine room and is wiping his hands on an oil-stained rag. Tiger tries a smile and a timid greeting. He gets no response and returns, self-consciously, to his writing. A title page is written with a flourish. A second page is given a number and a chapter heading. Donkeyman watches him for a few seconds then leaves.*

With eyes closed, pen poised, Tiger tries to recall as accurately as possible the photograph of his mother as a young girl.)

TIGER: All in white . . . everything was white . . . floppy sort of hat . . . with a broad brim . . . dress almost down to her ankles . . . a little necklace of beads around her throat . . . *(Betty appears. She is as he describes her. She stands expectantly still, posed for the camera)* . . . white gloves in one hand, a book in the other . . . old-fashioned shoes with buttons on the side . . . and stockings . . . also white . . . *(He pauses)*

BETTY: Go on.

TIGER *(Eyes still closed)*: I've left out something haven't I?

BETTY: Yes you have.

TIGER: What?

BETTY: I'm not going to tell you. You must guess.

TIGER: Ribbons? Ribbons on your hat?

BETTY: No.

TIGER: Some other jewelry . . . a broach . . . a bangle? . . .

BETTY: No.

TIGER: Damn it! I know there is something missing.

BETTY: Do you give up?

TIGER: No! Hat, dress, gloves, book . . . all right, what is it?

BETTY: You forgot the rose.

TIGER: Of course! At your waist . . . on your belt!

BETTY: That's right.

TIGER *(Opens his eyes)*: Yes, there it is. Still, I didn't do too badly. Only missed one item. I got everything else right.

BETTY: I expected you to get full marks.

TIGER: You did?

BETTY: Of course. You spent enough time there in the bedroom staring at me.

TIGER: Did I really?

BETTY: Oh yes. I've watched you grow up, standing there in front of me . . . staring . . . staring. You left quite a few grubby fingerprints on the glass to prove it. *(Pause)* You mean you don't remember?

TIGER: No, of course I do. I can even remember the very first time I saw you . . . really saw you I mean . . . you know, when you stopped being just another old family picture on the wall.

BETTY: I'm listening.

TIGER: I was alone in the house and I had sneaked into my parents bedroom to scratch through their drawers and cupboards to see what I could find. I knew that big people had all sorts of strange things hidden away from us children. Suddenly I heard a noise—I looked around quickly, thinking somebody was coming and there you were . . . on the wall, watching me. God, was it creepy! You looked so real, so alive, as if you could speak and were going to give me a rowing for what I was doing.

BETTY: You deserved it. You were being naughty.

TIGER: So? Seven years old. Everybody gets up to a few pranks at that age. It's healthy.

BETTY: But finish your story.

TIGER: I have.

BETTY: No you haven't. Before you left the room you came and stood in front of me and pulled faces at me.

TIGER: That's right. Because you knew. You knew what I got up to when I was left alone in the house. There was even a chance you might tell on me. Yes! That's how real you were for me. All my mother's stories about growing up in Middelburg has made you a very real presence in my life. You were walking around in my imagination long before today.

What were you like? . . . I used to ask myself. What secrets did you have? What did you dream about? What were you frightened of? One day I concentrated on just your physical presence. What it would be like to be really close to you, close enough to be able to look into your eyes, to see them blink. Close enough to even smell you! I got quite excited by that. I imagined a little aura of delicate, young, feminine odors . . . perfume maybe. Lavender! My mom's favorite. What would you say to an occasional little dab of old English lavender?

BETTY: If you say so.

TIGER: If I say so! Brilliant! That is . . . simply brilliant. That is what it is going to be all about isn't it . . . If I Say So! Creative authority. That's what you've put your finger on young lady. The freedom and authority of the creative artist to go in any direction his imagination chooses.

Okay. Enough stalling. Let's begin the big adventure. *(Pause)* Any ideas?

BETTY: About what?

TIGER: The opening. That all important first paragraph. You know . . . "Once upon a time, in a small Karoo town there was . . ." etc., etc.

BETTY: Who?

TIGER: You. Elizabeth Magdalena Katerina Potgieter.

BETTY: That's my name?

TIGER: Yes. My mother's maiden name.

BETTY: Say it again.

TIGER: Elizabeth Magdalena Katerina . . . Potgieter.

(Betty doesn't like it.)

Yes, I see what you mean. It's not very . . . it doesn't come lightly off the tongue. We need something with a little bit more air and less earth in it. A bit more style. Let's see . . . Elizabeth Joubert? No. Cronje? Rossouw? Elizabeth Rossouw! Not bad. It's the French you see.

Or Le Roux. Elizabeth Le Roux. I think we've got it.
Betty Le Roux!

BETTY: Can't I have an English name?

TIGER: No! You're an Afrikaner.

BETTY: Then I prefer Elizabeth Magdalena Katerina . . .

TIGER: Too late! I've decided. Remember what you said: "If
I say so!" Well I am saying you are Betty Le Roux.

BETTY *(Reluctantly)*: Betty Le Roux.

TIGER: You must remember this is going to be a novel, not a
biography. I will be taking a lot of liberties, young lady,
so the sooner you get used to it, the better.

    So how do we kick off? What is Miss Betty Le Roux
up to? What is she doing?

BETTY *(Resuming her pose for the camera)*: Waiting.

TIGER: For what?

BETTY: The camera.

TIGER *(Inspiration)*: For the flash of the camera! Betty Le
Roux, all in white, in the photographer's studio, waiting for the flash of the camera! We've got *it*! *(Very
excited)* We set the scene with a description of the studio . . . you know, the old-fashioned camera and everything . . . "Standing in the middle of the room like a
black-hooded, three-legged, wooden spider . . ." And
then you, posed and waiting. We'll make it your birthday . . . *(Betty wants to say something)* . . . Don't interrupt, it's all coming . . . your birthday . . . that's the
reason for the photograph—

BETTY: I want to be fifteen.

TIGER: Too young. You're seventeen. First stirrings of
womanhood and all that . . . "Her firm young body full
of strange and disturbing yearnings." *(Excited laughter)* The damn thing is running away with me! After
studio you go home— *(Pause. She does not share his
excitement)* Now what's the matter?

BETTY: I'm nervous.

TIGER: Of what?

BETTY: The Big Adventure
TIGER: Why?
BETTY: I don't know. It just makes me nervous.
TIGER: That's perfectly natural. We can even use it— "... A little undercurrent of anxiety about her future." But don't worry. If it all works out the way I've planned it, there's a happy ending in store for you.

(Pause.)

Don't you trust me?
BETTY: Can I? It's going to be my life you know.
TIGER: Yes, I do know! And I want to celebrate it. I want the world to know, love and respect Betty Potgieter—
BETTY *(Correcting him)*: Betty Le Roux! See what I mean. Even you aren't so sure about things.
TIGER: That was a slip of the tongue. We'll get used to your new name and so will the world. You've got to trust me, Betty. We'll get nowhere if you don't.
BETTY *(Still uncertain)*: All right.
TIGER: So after the photographer's studio and an introduction to the family— "... A humble but upright Afrikaner family ..." —mother in the kitchen, father reading the bible, sisters and brothers, the special relationship you have with one brother—he's the only person who really understands you, he knows that you are somehow different from the rest of them, you confide in him ...

(Tiger is now at his table writing furiously. Betty disappears. Donkeyman comes on deck with a mug of tea. He has washed and put on clean clothes. Again, he settles down at a distance from Tiger but he is obviously interested in what the young man is doing. Tiger stops writing and counts pages. He tries another greeting and smile.)

Twelve pages! Not a bad start. If I can keep going at this rate . . . who knows? . . . I might even have a first draft by the time we reach Japan. *(No response from Donkeyman)* You speak English? No speak English? Parlez vous Francais? Je parle un petit peu. No? Oh well, sorry, that's the best I can do.

(Tiger settles down and continues writing, his pen moving rapidly across the page, which soon joins the stack of those already done. He launches into yet another, but after a few lines he crumples it up, throws it away and starts again. Donkeyman's interest gets the better of him. He moves closer and watches Tiger and his pen with fascination.)

DONKEYMAN: What you do?

TIGER: So you do speak little English, hey. Very good.

DONKEYMAN *(Refers to Tiger's writing)*: Nini hii?

TIGER: What is it?

DONKEYMAN *(Nodding)*: Ndiyo.

TIGER: This, amigo, is the beginning of what I hope is going to be a good novel. You know—book? Big fat book? Like story? This him.

   You work down below? In engine room?

DONKEYMAN: Me Donkeyman.

TIGER: Donkeyman?

DONKEYMAN: Ndiyo.

TIGER: Is him your name?

DONKEYMAN *(Angrily)*: Donkeyman work.

TIGER: I see. Is your job.

DONKEYMAN: Ndiyo. Donkeyman job.

TIGER: Me work on bridge. Look after Captain my job. They call him my job—Captain's Tiger. So . . . *(Holds out his hand. Donkeyman shakes it reluctantly)* Tiger very happy meet Donkeyman.

(Tiger produces a tin of cigarette butts and cigarette papers. A fascinated Donkeyman watches him tear open the butts, sort out and discard the burnt tobacco and then roll a cigarette with what is left. He lights it and smokes. Tiger luxuriates in his interest.)

Beggars can't be choosers. No money.

DONKEYMAN *(Pointing to the manuscript)*: What you say? Soma!

TIGER: You like me read? *(Donkeyman nods. Tiger takes the page and reads)* "Hanging on the walls in an impressive array of ornate gilt frames were photographic portraits of the good citizens of this proud little town: sober young men in smart suits with starched chin-high white collars and waxed mustaches. Facing them on the opposite wall and also buttoned up to the chin, a bevy of attractive, but equally serious, young maidens. There were also formal bridal groups in wedding outfits and golden anniversary couples—the old men bearded and fierce, the old women thin-lipped and disapproving. Waiting now to join them—waiting for the flash from the old, wooden, tripod camera that stood in the middle of the room like a black-hooded spider, the flash that would forever fix in celluloid her fine-boned delicate features—stood young Betty Le Roux . . . and like all the others, she wasn't smiling."

(Tiger is very proud of his efforts.)

Is good? Is plenty good, amigo . . . even if I have to say so myself.

(In a sudden excess of high spirits, a wild surge of faith in himself and life, he declaims extravagantly) Life, Liberty and Love! That's what it's all about. That's the battle cry! You think I'm mad, don't you? I can't help it man. It's just so damned exciting, you

know, this huge adventure we call Life. Look out there Donkeyman . . . an ocean for God's sake! Look up . . . the heavens! You ever seen so many stars? And here in the middle of it all, me and you, sailing through a sultry tropical night into the future. And that future? Who knows what it holds. I'm telling you man, I get drunk just thinking about it. You agree? *(Donkeyman's nod could be read as agreement)* Put it there pardner. *(They shake once again)*

(Tiger perches himself on the hatch next to Donkeyman) But seriously now, if somebody had told me back home, in little old Port Elizabeth, that one day I would be sitting here on number four hatch of the SS *Graigaur*, next to "Donkeyman," headed for Aden, then Colombo, then Singapore, then Japan, and after that God alone knows where . . . I would have said they were crazy. But here we are! And we're in good company you know. Melville, Conrad, Hemingway, Faulkner, Twain—they all did it. Cut loose and took their chance with fate. There's no other way. You can't play it safe if you want to be a writer.

(Pause.)

Me from South Africa, Donkeyman. You? Your home? Where Donkeyman's kya?

DONKEYMAN: Afrika.

TIGER: That's the one! The Dark Continent. Me hitchhike all the up Africa. *(He demonstrates thumbing a lift)*

DONKEYMAN: Ah! Lifti!

TIGER: That's it. Lifti. Me Lifti Capetown to Cairo—all the way. Rhodesia, Nyasaland, Tanganyika . . .

DONKEYMAN: Kenya.

TIGER: Ah! You Kenya.

DONKEYMAN: Me m'Swahili.

TIGER: Kenya very nice place. Very nice people.

DONKEYMAN: Mombasa.

TIGER: Mombasa hey. Me no see Mombasa. After Tanganyika me go Congo, Sudan, Nile River . . . Juba, Kosti, Khartoum. Hard times, Donkeyman. No money, no food, no place sleep. But now SS *Graigaur* . . . nice bed, fully belly and I meet Donkeyman. How you say friend in Swahili?

DONKEYMAN: Rafiki.

TIGER: You me . . . rafiki?

DONKEYMAN: Sawa

TIGER: Tiger very happy now.

(A silence. They stare out into the night.)

DONKEYMAN: Kwaheri Afrika!

TIGER: Kwaheri?

(Donkeyman explains the meaning with a good-bye wave.)

Ah! Good-bye. Yep. It's that all right. Maybe long no see again hey.

DONKEYMAN: Ndiyo. *(Starting to leave)* Go sleep.

TIGER: Okay. Tomorrow night you come we talk some more. Hey Donkeyman! How you say good night in Swahili?

DONKEYMAN: Lala Salama.

TIGER: Lala Salama.

(Donkeyman leaves.)

SCENE 3

Another letter home.

TIGER:

Dear Mom,

Another letter chock-a-block with good news. Firstly, I've made a friend. He is most probably the fiercest looking black man in Africa, but don't start worrying now because he is in fact a jolly good bloke. He works down below in the engine room. Tell Dad he is what is called a Donkeyman. That will give him a chuckle. My other good news is that there are now sixty-nine pages of fairly legible handwriting stacked up on the table. I promise you, Mom, you won't be disappointed when one day you read: "Betty Le Roux. The Story of a South African Woman." Intact in her soul are all those secret dreams and ambitions of your youth.

I'll be posting this letter in Colombo.

Signing off on a balmy night
out in the Indian Ocean,
The Captain's Tiger

(He pauses.)

P.S. Tell Dad I haven't forgotten him. He'll be getting his own letter very soon.

SCENE 4

Betty appears. She now wears a simple but bright summer frock. Her reserve and caution of the first scene are gone—

she is full of life and eager for the next development in her story. She and Tiger are also more relaxed with each other.

BETTY: I don't know how I'm going to get through everything today. *(Ticking off the items on her fingers)* First there's a visit to the library to change my book. I finished the one on Florence Nightingale late last night. It's the most wonderful story I've ever read. I couldn't go to sleep afterwards—just lay in bed thinking about her and wondering if I would ever have the courage to do what she did, dedicate my life to alleviating the suffering of others. When I give it back I'm going to ask Mrs. Conradie to recommend some other books on self-sacrifice. I want to make a real study of it. Then it's a trip to the dentist with Hansie—that tooth has got to come out. And after that the shopping list my mother gave me, and if there's time on the way back home, I want to stop at Mrs. Vermeulens. She wants me to help her pick and arrange flowers for the big Fitzhenry wedding this weekend.

TIGER: Hold your horses, Miss Le Roux! They are running away with you.

BETTY: I can't help it. If I don't hurry I'll never get everything done. There's also my friend Mathilda. I promised her we'd go for a long walk this afternoon and share secrets. It's ages since we've had one of our heart-to-heart talks. And if I can squeeze it in—

TIGER: No you can't. Today is reserved for something else, something rather special.

BETTY: Why? What's going to happen?

TIGER: The buildup of emotional pressures inside you is going to lead to one of the pivotal moments in your life.

BETTY: Goodness me.

TIGER: Yes, this is the big one. You are going to realize that the time has come to leave the village.

(Pause.)

BETTY: So soon?

TIGER: Is that all you can say about the moment when you embrace your personal destiny for the first time? And I don't know if I would describe sixty-nine pages of a rough draft as being "So soon." You knew it was coming. You've had any number of conversations with Hansie about it.

BETTY: I know, but I'm still so happy in the village. I don't know if I really want to go yet. Can't we wait until I'm bored or . . .

TIGER: No. That would make the decision too easy. There's no conflict then and that is what we need. Conflict and resolution.

One part of you doesn't want to leave the safe little world you've grown up in, and then that other part of you with its secret vision of a life of action and purpose that knows that to make that vision come true you have to pack your suitcase and buy a second-class train ticket to Port Elizabeth. Look at Florence Nightingale. She packed up and went from England to the Crimea!

BETTY *(Reluctantly)*: Well I suppose . . . if you say so . . .

TIGER: Yes, I do. Come on, Betty, I thought you were going to trust me? Where's that spirit of adventure we explored in Chapter Two? Remember? That daredevil streak in your nature that was always getting you and Hansie into trouble. Another chapter of village gossip and Hansie's toothache and our reader is going to start yawning.

BETTY: It's easy for you to talk. All you've got to do is just scribble it down. I'm the one who has got to do it.

TIGER: Oh! I just talk and scribble it all down do I? Well Let me tell you Betty Le Roux that I happen to know what I'm talking and scribbling about! Yes. I've been up against it as well. I wouldn't be here on this ship . . .

you wouldn't be here. No, its even more basic than that—you wouldn't *be*, full stop, if I hadn't faced up to my moment of decision as well. And for your information I didn't have a suitcase and a train ticket and a loving Hansie on the platform with a little basket of cold lamb chops and brown bread for the journey, and waving me good-bye when the train pulled away.

A couple of tins of sardines and one change of clothes in an old haversack, and then out onto the National Road to wait for "lifti." Cairo here I come!

BETTY: Weren't you frightened?

TIGER: You bet I was. Scared as hell! I was a mess inside. I hadn't even gotten my first lift and I was already starting to feel homesick. That's how bad it was. But I also knew I had no choice. I had to do it. Ever since I was small there's been this feeling inside me, a sort of yearning for something I couldn't name or put into words. I could never see clearly what it was I wanted—it was just there, this . . . this longing for it. The only thing I knew for sure was that I would never find it at home. So you've got to leave. That's all there is to it. You've got to go out there and try to find it because all the time that feeling is there inside you, like a bird in a cage wanting to be free. So here I am . . . on my way to Japan.

BETTY: All right then. What do you want me to do?

TIGER: It's going to be very simple to start with. We don't want our reader to know what's coming. You're going for a walk in the veld . . .

BETTY: Can Mathilda come?

TIGER: No. No Mathilda! No Hansie! Nobody. You want to be alone, you want to get away from everybody because that little bird inside you is beating its wings, very desperately, against the bars of the cage.

(Betty disappears.)

21

SCENE 5

Tiger and Donkeyman. Tiger is writing furiously. Donkeyman is fixing the broken strap of a sandal. After a few seconds Tiger puts down his pen, sits back and takes a deep breath.

TIGER: Okay. Are you ready?

DONKEYMAN: Ndiyo.

TIGER *(Reading from his manuscript)*: ". . . Gathering up her skirts and laughing aloud at herself, she skipped lightly over the last few yards of broken rock to the summit of the koppie. With her heart pounding from both her exertions and a sense of triumph at having made it to the top, she settled down on a warm rock to regain her breath. Spread out in front of her was a view of the Karoo in all its glory—a landscape of muted purples and browns, and dusty distances. Overhead, wheeling majestically in the vast sky, sole ruler of that infinity of space and light, was a black eagle. It's wild, desolate cry quickened her pulse. It seemed to be calling her, calling, urging her also to be free and conquer the world. Betty stood up, and in a loud, clear voice called back: 'I hear you and I understand.' She knew the time had come to leave."

(A few seconds of speechless admiration for his own writing.)

Heavy stuff hey! *(Pounding his heart with a fist)* Big feeling here. Tiger write okay.

DONKEYMAN *(Muttering to himself)*: Eebwana una seema ni ni.

TIGER *(He reads again)*: ". . . A landscape of muted purples and browns, and dusty distances . . ." Ja! Trouble is Tiger write too much okay. Make himself homesick.

DONKEYMAN: En de leah.

TIGER: Donkeyman also? You wanting sometimes go back home? Go back Kenya?

(Donkeyman doesn't answer, he stares into space.)

You got wife Donkeyman? . . . Babies? . . . You know, bambinos. Picaninnies?

DONKEYMAN: No, no wife . . . no mine. Utando wamadati-so—is difficult—sweat, toil, I drift on. I was boy like you, but life turn me into man. Father far away, three sisters, work is all me understand. No wife.

TIGER: Me also. Tiger no get married. Wife and babies no good for writing life. Tiger need freedom. But it's crazy isn't it. One part of you hears the eagle and takes up the challenge and another part of you just wants to call it a day and go back home. And I nearly did! Ja. Tiger nearly no sit here tonight. It was touch and go my friend, one day back there in the Congo. Donkeyman know Congo? Belgian Congo?

DONKEYMAN *(Mapping Africa in the air with a finger)*: Kenya, Tanganyika, Uganda, Congo.

TIGER: That's it. Well there . . . *(Putting his finger on Donkeyman's map)* . . . Congo . . . one time Tiger him sit five days waiting lifti. Nothing come. Five days!

(The memory comes to him) Five stinking days on the side of the road outside a scabby little village, with all its inhabitants on the other side having a wonderful time watching a white man's misery. First day I just braved it out: on my legs all the time—pacing, reciting poetry, trying very unsuccessfully not to notice them. Second day I spent on my backside like them, trying to stare them out. That wasn't such a good idea. They started laughing at me. Third day I decided to use my time constructively. I gave them a lecture on existentialism.

(The Lecture:)

"Briefly defined it is a school of thought based on a conception of the absolute inanity of existence, the absurdity of the universe and the negation of all creation . . . and if you want proof of that I suggest you examine our present situation: one solitary and desperate white man waiting for nothing, and all of you with nothing better to do than to sit there on your backsides and watch him waiting for nothing."
The fourth day I spent mostly crying. No kidding. Pulled my varsity blazer over my head and cried like a baby. And then on the fifth day, lo and behold! the devil appeared! How do I know he was the devil? Simple. He was driving a big lorry, he was all by himself, he had a case of ice-cold beers on the seat next to him, and—wait for it!—he was going the wrong way— Back!

My friend, you were that close *(The smallest possible distance between thumb and forefinger)* to not having the pleasure of my company. So why didn't I climb aboard and go back? *(Shakes his head)* Belgian devil give Tiger beer me drink him. Boy oh boy was it good—me happy happy and talk talk with devil. Me drink two beer—still happy happy and more talk talk. Me drink three beer—Tiger feel sick, go bush, vomit vomit. Tiger come back—lorry gone!

(Tiger produces his little hoard of cigarette stubs, piece of brown paper and starts to roll a cigarette. He identifies the cigarettes as he tears them open.)

First Officer, filter tip . . . this one?—ah, Players! Maybe Chief Engineer or Radio Officer, him also smoke Players. This one—Woodbine—Third Officer . . .

(Donkeyman gets up suddenly and leaves.)

You Turning in? Hey . . . Lala Salama.

(Donkeyman doesn't respond. Tiger is alone for a few seconds. Donkeyman returns and places a new, unopened, round tin of fifty Woodbine cigarettes on the card table in front of Tiger.)

For me? Hell! Donkeyman! . . .

(Tiger is for once speechless. He opens the tin carefully, takes out a cigarette and treats it like a fine Havana cigar: smells it, lights it and then, like a man with a million pounds in the bank, sits back in his chair and stretches out his legs. He takes a deep drag and blows smoke rings. Donkeyman enjoys a huge laugh and settles down again on the hatch. Tiger's fountain pen, lying idle and open on the table, is irresistible. After a few seconds of hesitation, Donkeyman picks it up carefully and examines it, testing the sharpness of the nib with a finger. Tiger watches him.)

DONKEYMAN: Peni ya wino. Swahili word for him. Peni ya wino.
TIGER: You want to try? *(Pushing forward a blank sheet of paper)* Go on, write . . . andika. Write him your name.
DONKEYMAN *(Hurriedly abandoning the pen)*: No andika— no kusoma.
TIGER: Donkeyman no read no write?
DONKEYMAN: Sawa.
TIGER: No go school?
DONKEYMAN: No skooli. All time Donkeyman get big big no skooli no titcha. Working all time fishboti—me fiksi injini. All time working working—Malindi, Mombasa—no time do nuting, only fiksi injini for fish-

boti. So one time Mama say: Musa, is no good big boy no read no write. So Donkeyman try—find titcha in skooli and try hard. *(Drawing the letters clumsily in the air)* A . . . B . . . G . . . No good. Titcha take him my *(Indicates his hand)* my mkono—Whack! Whack! Try again. A . . . B . . . G . . . No good. Titcha come whack! Whack! Little boy for skooli laugh laugh. All time laugh for me, so one time Donkeyman fucking fed up now and had enough, I go back and tell Mama is bullshit—book bullshit; Mama, penselli bullshit; Mama, skooli bullshit; Mama and little boy laughing for me. And Mama say: "Musa, you go back fiksi injini for fishboti."

All time I say bullshit. Newspaypah, magazetti—all things paypah—no use for me. All time Donkeyman happy fiksi injini and mota. Den one time Tiger come. Donkeyman watch him Tiger andika. Wow! Peni ya wino like motaboti. Upisiupesi!! *(Taking the pen and demonstrating the speed of Tiger's writing)* Everyday Tiger andika. Donkeyman tink Aha! What dis now? Den Tiger read paypah. Donkeyman no fahamu good all what Tiger say *(Tapping his head)* but Donkeyman see what Tiger read make Tiger feel plenty happy. Donkeyman tink again, Aha! Maybe dis one is no bullshit. Donkeyman know spanner, bisbisi, screwidriver, monkiwrench, but him? . . . *(Refers to the fountain pen. He shakes his head and puts it back respectfully on the table)*

TIGER: So okay. Maybe Donkeyman no andika, but Donkeyman help Tiger andika.

DONKEYMAN: Donkeyman help Tiger?

TIGER: Donkeyman help Tiger plenty plenty. When Donkeyman watch Tiger andika, Tiger feel strong. When Tiger read story and Donkeyman listen, Tiger feel more strong. This one *(Hand on his manuscript)* Tiger and Donkeyman andika this one together. You and me.

(Twining together his fore and middle finger to make his point. Holds up his manuscript) This one is not bullshit. One day this one is big big book, and when I send him to Donkeyman I write in it: To my friend and comrade Donkeyman who so helped me write these words on the Rock of Gold.

DONKEYMAN: Is good.

TIGER: Is very good.

(The coauthorship is sealed with a handshake. Donkeyman starts to leave.)

DONKEYMAN: Lala Salama.

TIGER: No wait. Donkeyman how you say "thank you" in Swahili?

DONKEYMAN: Nashukuru.

TIGER: And plenty plenty?

DONKEYMAN: Sana.

TIGER *(Holding up the tin of cigarettes)*: Nashukuru sana rafiki. Lala salama.

(Donkeyman stares at Tiger for a few seconds, then leaves.)

SCENE 6

Another letter home.

TIGER:

Dear Mom,
    We reached Colombo last night. It was already dark when we dropped anchor. I could see the lights of the town in the distance, strung out like a glittering neck-lace along the shore. All around us were the lights of other ships also at anchor in the roadstead.

I went to bed and dreamt about home.

Early this morning, just before sunrise, I was back on deck. There was a soft mist on the water, and floating in it, their huge bulks softened by the swirling vapors, more ships of more shapes and sizes than I had ever imagined were sailing the seven seas.

(Donkeyman comes up behind Tiger and they stare into the distance. Tiger is openmouthed with wonder and awe, and Donkeyman nods his head—he has seen it many times. Tiger is counting the ships.)

. . . Twenty-five, twenty-six, twenty-seven . . . and there's still all those over there—and there! Just look at them, man! That one . . . she's as big as a bloody cathedral. Can you read the name? O-ron-say?

DONKEYMAN: Sawa. P ana O.

TIGER: You know him, Donkeyman?

DONKEYMAN: Donkeyman know him. *(He points to another ship)* British India. Good money for pay that one, good food. *(Another ship)* Sykes Lines. American. Good money also.

TIGER: How would you even begin to describe it? A spectacle—a panorama—that's a good one! "Spread out before their wondering eyes a panoramic vision of the commerce of the seas." *(Pounds his heart with his fist)* Big feeling inside. Tiger want to laugh, Tiger want to sing, Tiger want to cry . . . all mix up. I mean—it's Colombo for God's sake. Ceylon! An ancient civilization! The pearl of the Indian Ocean! I am going to see a new world. Donkeyman also happy?

DONKEYMAN: Donkeyman plenty happy. Tonight hot fish curry and a good fuck.

TIGER: Wow!

DONKEYMAN: Sawa. Wow!

28

TIGER: Hot fish curry and a good fuck. Yep. That sounds like an interesting time all right. Donkeyman know Colombo.

DONKEYMAN: Me know Colombo plenty good. Plenty time come here. You walk in street, Ceylon boy stop you: "Hey sailor, five rupee you jig-a-jig my sister."

TIGER: Aha! You call him jig-a-jig?

DONKEYMAN: Sawa. You come Tiger. I show. Okay?

TIGER: You want me go jig-a-jig with you?

DONKEYMAN: Sawa. You and me. Tonight.

TIGER *(Panic)*: No—good heavens—no, no. Me too much work, plenty, plenty writing. Heaven's yes—plenty busy andika with peni ya wino. Me no go tonight. And anyway when me go ashore, me must first look him Buddha temple . . . plenty big special one for him here in Colombo. Plenty historic building Captain tell me—interesting architecture from the colonial period, also botanical gardens. Yep. Tiger him got plenty things to see. Jig-a-jig come later.

(His voice trails away into silence. Pause. Back to the ships.)

What was it . . . "Bathed in misty morning light a panoramic vista . . ."

(Pause.)

She pretty?

DONKEYMAN: Who?

TIGER: Sister for Ceylon boy.

DONKEYMAN: Plenty pretty.

TIGER: You old Romeo you! And nice and young hey.
(Illustrates his meaning with gestures)

DONKEYMAN *(He gets the meaning)*: Ah! Kijana. Also Mama you like Mama. Plenty sisters. Five rupee short time, twenty rupee jig-jig all night. Tiger come.

TIGER: No. Maybe some other time.

DONKEYMAN: Kwa-nini? Tiger no like jig-a-jig?

TIGER *(Bluster)*: Oh no . . . don't get me wrong . . . Tiger like jig-a-jig. Oh yes, is very nice. Very healthy. But there is a time and a place for everything . . . and this, dear rafiki, is the time for writing. *(Sits down with determination at his table and prepares for another session)*

DONKEYMAN *(Leaving)*: Okay. Tutaonana baadaye, Tiger.

TIGER: Mzuri.

SCENE 7

Tiger at his table, trying to write, and Betty. She is rebellious, angry and very emphatic.

BETTY: No! And I'll say it again—No! No! No!

TIGER: You can say it as many times as you like. I'm not listening to you.

BETTY: Well you had better. Don't think you can just scribble your way out of it. You won't silence me that way. It's my story and I'm telling you I don't like it.

TIGER *(Trying to ignore her. He closes his eyes as he struggles to shape a sentence)*: "But the thought that worried her most . . . the image that haunted and disturbed her most during these last few days in the village . . ."

BETTY: You're making me very cross. Don't ignore me. *(She takes the pen out of his hand, screws the top back on and puts it down on the table)* You are not going any further until you've dealt with it. *(She puts his manuscript down in front of him)* Find it and read it again.

TIGER: I don't need to. We've done it so many times already I know it by heart. *(Quoting)* "Gathering up her skirts and laughing aloud at herself, Betty skipped lightly . . ."

BETTY *(Hands to her ears)*: Not aloud! To yourself. It's too embarrassing.

(Pause.)

Well?

TIGER: Well what?

BETTY: Did you squirm?

TIGER: No.

BETTY: Not even a blush of embarrassment?

TIGER: No . . . *(Betty throws up her arms in a helpless gesture)* . . . and the reason I didn't is because I happen to think that those few pages are the best in the whole manuscript.

BETTY: I give up.

TIGER: God, I wish you would.

BETTY: No I won't. My credibility is at stake. If you leave that section in, everybody will laugh at me. Nobody will believe a word of what follows.

TIGER *(Collecting himself)*: Okay. The only way to settle the matter is for us to try and discuss it in a calm and rational manner. So no more vindictive sarcasm please. What is wrong with it?

BETTY: It's false. It's exaggerated. It's sentimental. It's—

TIGER: One at a time please. What is false about it? Don't just throw out wild judgments like that. Show me specifically—

BETTY: I'm not finished. We agreed that I was going to go for a quiet walk in the veld so that I could think things over.

TIGER: And isn't that what we've got?—A quiet walk in the veld which on a sudden and perfectly natural impulse on your side becomes an easy little ramble to the top of a koppie.

BETTY: An easy little ramble? There is no such thing as an easy little ramble and skipping lightly to the top of a Karoo koppie. It usually takes hours of scrambling over rocks and big boulders with those terrible, little thorny bushes tearing your stockings to pieces. And when I do get to the top, what happens? I recite awful poetry and sing arias to eagles . . .

TIGER *(Trying very hard to control himself)*: I thought we were going to discuss this in a calm—

BETTY *(Ignoring him)*: False, exaggerated, sentimental and improbable.

TIGER: Are you finished?

BETTY: And dangerous. Summertime. Snakes . . . not to talk about broken ankles.

TIGER *(Defeated)*: This time I give up. *(Puts away his fountain pen. The session is over)*

BETTY *(Unperturbed)*: Good. Do you want me to go?

TIGER *(Back into the fray)*: I know it's a big . . . heroic image . . . but that's a deliberate choice. That is what I wanted, what the moment needs, what the story is all about—the Karoo woman as Hero, which is what my mother would have been if life had given her half a chance. You and Olive Schreiner. Do you know where Olive is buried? At the top of a Karoo koppie in the Cradock district! I've made the pilgrimage. And what is more I saw and heard a black eagle when I was up there. That's where the idea comes from. I didn't just suck it out of my thumb. There's even a veiled allusion to Olive's novel in our subtitle: "The story of a South African Woman." What's the matter with you? Why can't you see it? It all fits together so perfectly.

BETTY: Are you finished? Can I go now?

TIGER: No! You also seem to forget that this is only a first draft. There'll be plenty of time later to trim it and tone it down . . . if that is necessary!

(Nothing from Betty.)

All right. So then tell me, very simply, exactly what it is you want.

BETTY: I want to be real. I want a real life.

TIGER: Am I not giving you that?

BETTY: No. That scene on the koppie is not real.

TIGER: Well the way it "really" happened is not very exciting you know. One of my mother's aunts from Port Elizabeth came to visit them in Middelburg and when she saw how hard-up the family was she suggested that young Betty should go back with her to Port Elizabeth and look for a job. I mean . . . how boring can you get!

BETTY: I like it. It sounds real.

TIGER: But there's no drama in it. No sense of personal destiny. Of you being "the master of your fate, the captain of your soul." Try to understand that my job as a writer is to make reality dramatic, and to do that I have to take liberties. I warned you about all this right at the beginning.

BETTY: I don't mind you taking a few "liberties." I object to being violated.

TIGER: That's strong language.

BETTY: I know, and its deliberate.

TIGER: And what if I exercise my authority?

BETTY: You mean . . . "If you say so"?

TIGER: Yes.

BETTY: I wouldn't do that if I were you.

TIGER: Why not?

BETTY: Because I'll leave you.

TIGER: What do you mean?

BETTY *(Calmly)*: I can't say it any simpler. I'll leave you. When you want me again, I won't be there.

TIGER: Just like that!

BETTY: Yes.

TIGER *(Disbelief)*: You would leave me? After all we've been through? No you wouldn't.

BETTY: Yes I would.

TIGER: For how long?

BETTY: That is for you to discover.

TIGER *(Appalled)*: You really mean that don't you?

BETTY: Yes.

(He sees Betty in a new light.)

TIGER: All right. I'll rewrite.

(Betty disappears.)

SCENE 8

Another letter home.

TIGER:
Dear Mom,
We're at sea again, and thank god for that. For a variety of reasons Colombo was a very frustrating experience. Just when I thought I was getting the hang of things I had to tear up no less than thirteen pages. I console myself with the knowledge that its a good sign—any writer worth his salt always savages his manuscript. Its part of the process. If you don't, the critics will. But don't worry, Mom, your story will be told. That remains a solemn promise. Even with those thirteen gone there are still one hundred and thirty-two pages of it on my table. Our next port of call is Singapore, where we take on bunkers and supplies, and then head for Japan, the port of Niigata. The Captain has warned me that after Singapore the weather is going to get very cold . . .

SCENE 9

The sick bay. Tiger, bundled up in a blanket, with his manuscript. Donkeyman with mugs of hot cocoa.

TIGER *(Reading)*: "Belching smoke and sparks into the dark, star-filled, Karoo night, the locomotive thundered on like a raging black behemoth out of Africa's ancient past. Lying warm and snug in her second-class bunk, Betty allowed the train's clattering rhythm to lull and soothe her fears about the uncertain future that lay ahead of her. There was something comfortingly familiar about the repetitive clatter. After a few minutes she realized what it was—the train was rattling out the rhythm of her name:

Betty Le Roux
Betty Le Roux
Clickety-clack
Clickety-clack.

With a little laugh at herself and her fears, she snuggled deeper into her blankets, closed her eyes and drifted off to sleep."

(Donkeyman examines the manuscript with pride.)

One hundred and sixty-eight . . . not out! That's a good partnership. Won't be long before we've got two hundred up on the scoreboard.
(Tiger makes notes) Next we move on to . . . let's see . . . yes, here we are: ". . . Early morning arrival in Port Elizabeth—crowded station scene. Describe. Finds her way through city to aunt's house in Sydenham.

"Next day starts looking for work. First job: waitress in the Rand Café in Jetty Street—a dangerous world of prostitutes and sailors. Betty leaves aunt's house and moves into room above café. End chapter with the sound of music drifting in through the open window—Mom's story about listening to Dad playing the piano."

(Notebook down.)

It's a pivotal scene and I'm going to write it exactly as she told me. No frills, no liberties.

She hated the job—on her legs all the time, difficult customers sending back food or arguing about the bill, drunk sailors trying to feel her up, prostitutes teasing her. At the end of the day she would go upstairs to her little room, open the window and then collapse on her bed and lie there in the dark, listening to the music of a handsome young man playing the piano in the hotel lounge across the alleyway. She could actually see him from her window. It's perfect isn't it. If I had made that up people would say it was too much, that things like that don't happen in real life. Well they're wrong. It did. That's how she first saw him. My Dad.

(Pause. They drink cocoa.)

DONKEYMAN: Why you write, Tiger?

TIGER: What do you mean?

DONKEYMAN: So much you write. All the time . . . write, write . . . one paypah, one paypah, one paypah—look . . . now is plenty paypah. Why?

TIGER: Me write Donkeyman because . . . *(Pause)* . . . from time when Tiger was small small Bambino Tiger very much like words. All the time, play with words. No good play rugby, cricket, football. No good play with other boys. Also no good play with girls. Just about no good everything. But when Tiger read him the book or make him the story, Tiger feel . . . strong, Tiger feel safe.

So what Donkeyman say?

DONKEYMAN *(Handing back the manuscript)*: Donkeyman say is good Tiger write.

TIGER: Why is good?

DONKEYMAN: When Tiger write Donkeyman feel . . . *(He doesn't know the English word for what he wants to say)* . . . kubwa . . . muhimu . . .

TIGER *(Guessing)*: Happy? No. *(Donkeyman tries to explain with gestures and Tiger tries to interpret them)* Strong? Comfortable? *(More head shaking from Donkeyman. He stands up, pushes out his chest and slaps Tiger on the back)* Approving . . . congratulatory . . . *(He knows they are not right)*

DONKEYMAN *(Desperate)*: Sikiliza! *(He points to his ears)*

TIGER: Okay, I Listen.

DONKEYMAN: Sawa. You listen. *(Speaking carefully)* Tiger little brother for Donkeyman.

TIGER: I got you . . . which makes Donkeyman big brother for Tiger.

DONKEYMAN: Sawa! When big brother see little brother do big thing, do good thing . . . what big brother feel?

TIGER: When little brother do big thing, big brother feel . . . proud! That's the word you're looking for. Proud!

DONKEYMAN *(Finally satisfied. He makes a meal of the word)*: Proud! Sawa. When Tiger write, Donkeyman feel proud.

(He stands and stretches.)

Go sleep now. Two days . . . u Japani.

TIGER: Lala salama, big brother.

DONKEYMAN: Lala salama.

(Donkeyman leaves. Tiger pulls up his blanket and goes to sleep. The lights dim.)

SCENE 10

Tiger dreams. Betty, wearing a nightgown, comes drifting in to a background of soft piano music.

BETTY: Hello.

TIGER: What are you doing here?

BETTY: Just . . . visiting.

TIGER: In your nightie?

BETTY: I was restless. I couldn't sleep . . . and it's all your fault. It's all those strange and disturbing yearnings you've churned up in me. You don't seem very pleased to see me you know.

TIGER: Because this happens to be a private dream. I know I've got to put up with you when I'm working but not now. So please go away

BETTY: You're hurting my feelings.

TIGER: Good. That was my intention. Vamoose!

BETTY: Don't you want to dream about me?

TIGER: Definitely not. You give me a hard enough time when I'm awake. God alone knows what you'd get up to in a dream.

BETTY: And if I promise to behave?

TIGER: Good night. Put out the light when you leave.

BETTY: The light is already out. *(Tiger pulls the blanket over his head)* You won't get rid of me that way so stop behaving like a child.

TIGER: What do you want? Why are you here?

BETTY: I also want to dream.

TIGER: You can't.

BETTY: Yes I can. Just you wait and see.

TIGER: Don't you understand? This is already a dream. If you also start, where the hell are we going to end up? We might never get back to reality.

BETTY *(Ignoring him)*: I want to dream about that handsome young man playing the piano in the lounge of the Palmerston Hotel. Listen! Do you hear him? *(Singing softly)*

> Ramona,
> When day is done I hear you calling,
> Ramona . . .

TIGER: No! No! No! Hands off! I warn you now, if you start interfering with that scene.

BETTY *(She ignores him and continues singing)*:

> I'll always remember the rambling rose
> you wore in your hair . . .

I'm lying there on my bed in my nightgown. It's a warm summer's night. My young body is hot and sweating, my heart throbbing. His music is drifting in through the open window. It feels as if it's caressing me . . .

TIGER: That does it. I'm putting on the light.

BETTY: You can't. You're powerless. You can't move. *(He tries. He can't)* Waves of desire are passing over me. I put my hands on my young breasts . . .

TIGER *(Fingers in his ears)*: I'm not *listening.*

BETTY: Suddenly I see him there in the room, coming towards me—I open my arms . . .

TIGER: Stop! Stop!

BETTY: Don't interrupt me now! Can't you see what's happening?

TIGER: Only too clearly. And I am not prepared to go that far.

BETTY: Oh, I see! You are not prepared to go that far? Well that's just too bad because I am. And what's more I intend to go much further.

TIGER: Betty, I implore you—please!—just pause for a moment and think about the South African Board of Censors.

BETTY: I see. Lying there on my bed, on the point of giving myself body and soul to my very first embrace, you want me to pause—just for a moment!—and think about the South African Board of Censors.

TIGER: They'll never allow it.

BETTY: To hell with them. You're the author. Just write it!

TIGER: And never get published? Is that what you want? To be a bottom-drawer manuscript that somebody might discover in a hundred years time.

BETTY: So then will you please tell me Mr. Author what your plans were for me and my "strange and disturbing yearnings"? Chronic frustration for the sake of the South African Board of Censors? Anyway I think that bunch of old idiots is just a cover-up for something else. And I also think I know what that is. You! You're just stalling aren't you. And why in heaven's name? Sexual desire is a perfectly healthy and normal human drive. You're behaving as if you're scared of it.

TIGER: I'm not.

BETTY: Well that is what it looks like. Look at you! Shivering—

TIGER: It's cold.

BETTY: Anyone would think that you . . . *(Pause)*

TIGER: What?

BETTY: No. Good heavens! It couldn't be. *(Pause)* Or could it?

TIGER: I don't know what you're talking about.

BETTY: That you're avoiding the issue because you know nothing about it . . . and the reason for that is you are in fact still a virgin.

TIGER: Shut up! You know nothing about me.

BETTY: Then deny it. Come on. Tell me I'm wrong.

TIGER: You're wrong.

BETTY: No. I don't believe you! My God! Twenty years old and you're still a virgin? The Captain's Tiger is still a whelp. *(A good laugh which she cuts off abruptly)* No. It's not funny, it's outrageous! You had the nerve, the conceit, the male arrogance to think that in spite of your ignorance about the most basic drive in human nature you could write about me? Tell My Story? Make me fall in love, eavesdrop on my most private thoughts and feelings, peep through the keyhole at my most intimate scenes?

When we started out you stood there in front of me like a Mr. Know-All and said I must trust you—and I did! Well you had no right to ask for that trust. You would never have got me to go along with you if I had known the truth.

If you want my advice, Mr. Author, go back and tear up every page of your precious manuscript and start again after you've discovered what it means to hold a woman in your arms.

TIGER: It doesn't work like that!

BETTY: Oh it doesn't, does it. Am I in for another lecture on the theory and practice of great literature?

TIGER: Yes you are. Writers don't have to experience everything they write about. That's why we've got imaginations. So that we can escape the limitations of our own experience.

BETTY: God, I am so sick and tired of your nonsense. Out of all the would-be writers in the world I had to land up with you. You're trying to squirm out of it and it won't work. And stop talking to me about "we writers." Before you can even start to think about yourself as one you've got to be a man, which you aren't yet, my boy.

So just when were you going to do something about it? Your wedding night? *(Another good laugh)* This is a very serious situation you know. We can't go any further until you've done it. You can't lead me into the world of temptation and desire if you don't know the way. *(Drawing nearer)* Of course, there is a possible solution to our dilemma, you know. We could wander in there together, hand in hand, like the two innocents we are . . . discover and enjoy all its delights together . . .

TIGER: What are you suggesting?

BETTY *(Teasing)*: Oh come on, Mr. Author. Don't make me blush. Surely I don't have to spell it out. *(Sliding into bed beside him)* Use that famous imagination of yours. And for heaven's sake stop shivering! Look at me. I'm not frightened. And I know you want it every bit as much as I do.

TIGER *(Panic)*: For God's sake, no. Do you realize what you're doing? You're based on my mother. This is as good as incest! Donkeyman! Donkeyman!

(He breaks through his paralysis and escapes Betty.)

SCENE II

Number four hatch. Tiger and Donkeyman side-by-side looking at Japan as the ship steams into port.

DONKEYMAN: U Japani

TIGER: The Land of the Rising Sun is very very cold, big brother. Old Man say we stay here two weeks. Maybe three. Off-load salt. Fix engine. Look for new cargo. Plenty time see Niigata. You know him this place?

DONKEYMAN: Sawa. No curry but plenty good soup.

TIGER: And Japanese boy? Him got sister like Ceylon boy?

DONKEYMAN: Sawa. Also plenty good sisters. Japani jig-jig very good?

TIGER: Donkeyman go jig-jig.

DONKEYMAN: Sawa. You want also?

TIGER: Yes.

DONKEYMAN *(Slapping Tiger on the back and a good laugh)*: Is good. I take you. Tonight. I pay for you good Japanese sister.

SCENE 12

AUTHOR *(To the audience)*: Betty was right of course, and I knew it. Twenty years old and still a virgin? Nowadays a claim like that would make you a candidate for the *Guiness Book of Records*, but even back then that was pushing it. By the time we sailed into Niigata the prospect of my first full sexual experience had acquired huge symbolic significance. It was going to change everything you see—starting with *Me*. Imagine it for heaven's sake—a new Me!—bold, decisive, self-assured. Wouldn't you find the courage to jump off the high-diving board if that prospect presented itself? My timid little soul certainly did. When seven o'clock came I didn't need any persuading to crawl into a battered old taxi behind Donkeyman and drive off into the Japanese night.

Early the next morning I stood shivering outside the house in the Red Light District in which my initiation into manhood had taken place. There was snow on the ground and I was looking at a world, and a *me*, that hadn't changed very much, if at all. I had done it all right, but there I was . . . cold, hungry, bleary-eyed, hungover from a mixture of saki and Japanese whiskey, worrying about not getting back to the ship in time to serve the Captain his breakfast—that vague sense of guilt I always lived with still totally intact. It all felt very familiar. But, on the other hand, I'd also had a good time . . . to be honest with you, a damned good time. So the fact that the longed-for miracle—my personal transformation!—had not taken place was a little easier to accept. I shrugged off the disappointment as just another one of Life's dirty tricks, and settled down to enjoy the new world of pleasure my good friend Donkeyman had introduced me to.

Her name was Aiko. She was neither young nor pretty, but she made up for that in other ways. With infinite patience and exquisite tact, she gave me my first lessons in that most ancient and personal of all the arts: how to touch another human being.

To start with our relationship was the usual one of the Red Light District: hard cash in return for soft favors, but it turned into something more special when she became my partner in crime as well as in pleasure. You see, there was no way I could expect Donkeyman to go on financing my newly found appetite, which did most definitely grow by what it fed on. So, without any real qualms, I must confess, I started pilfering the ship's stores—soap, washing powder, tinned food, candles—anything I could get my hands on when nobody was looking. And the resourceful Aiko turned my loot into hard cash on Niigata's flourishing black market.

Forty-six years is a long time, too long for me now to put into correct order the jumble of images I have from those few weeks with her: cracking raw eggs into bowls of steaming soup in a little workman's eating house, my hopeless attempt at a serious conversation reducing her to hysterical laughter—she couldn't speak a word of English—or in her room, both of us suddenly silenced and looking up with frightened eyes as a big earth tremor set the lamp above our heads swinging like a pendulum.

Donkeyman and myself in adjoining wooden tubs of scalding hot water, being scrubbed down by the ladies before being allowed upstairs into their rooms. And waking up one night in her room, finding myself alone in the blankets on the floor, and just lying there listening to the soft murmuring voices of the Japanese sisters. They were talking softly in an adjoining room while their customers' slept.

Lying there I remembered the silkworms I used to keep in a shoe box when I was a little boy, and I remember thinking that if they could have whispered secrets to each other, that is what they would have sounded like.

There is however one image that I can place very accurately. It is the last one I have of her. Our ship is pulling away from its berth in the gray weather that was the color of all those Niigata days . . . and Aiko, heavily muffled against the cold, and framed by the double doors of a dockside warehouse, is standing very still watching the SS *Graigaur* sail away. She had given me a farewell present—beautiful calligraphy on a square of rice paper. I had it translated later: "All Life Is Learning."

SCENE 13

Number four hatch. The heat and lassitude of the Tropics. Tiger, at the card table, delaying tactics as he tries without success to settle down to a session of writing—cleaning fountain pen nib, arranging paper, repositioning table and chair, anything that will waste time and defer the moment when he must confront blank paper. Donkeyman, more sweaty and oil-stained than usual, comes on deck. He settles down on the hatch and starts to take apart and clean a badly rusted piece of machinery.

TIGER: How's it going? You fix engine?
DONKEYMAN: Not going. Boiler pressure still no good.

TIGER: Shit man, at this rate we'll never reach Fiji. What does the chief say?

DONKEYMAN: Him very angry. "Fucking useless boiler! Fucking rotten old ship!" Say he wash my hands of the whole fucking business. In his cabin now drinking cold beer.

TIGER: Oh Great! That will get the boiler pressure up.

DONKEYMAN: Chief right, Tiger. This ship too old now.

TIGER: Oh well, I'm quite happy to just drift around out here in the middle of nowhere for a day or two.

DONKEYMAN: So is plenty good time for you write.

TIGER: The doldrums! That's where we are you know. First Officer showed me in the chart room. We've broken down slap-bang on the equator. Not even so much as a degree off. Kind of ominous isn't it. Latitude zero degrees. Somebody on this ship has shot an albatross!

DONKEYMAN: I say is plenty good time for you write, Tiger.

TIGER: I heard you. And I'm getting there. Sometimes it helps to let your mind just wander off in any direction it likes. It sort of refreshes it. Open's it up to new ideas. And that is what my head needs right now, a refreshing surge of new ideas. *(Settles down once again at his table)* Japan too much good time. Make Tiger too excited. Concentration not so good at the moment. *(A pause for memories)* But by God it was worth it.

That could be another story you know, me and you, our Niigata nights! *(Pause for a decision. Lowering his voice and beckoning Donkeyman closer)* Tiger tell Donkeyman big secret. First time for me. Yep. First time for Tiger, jig-jig with girl. But what really amazed me, man, was how simple it turned out to be. Because, I'll be honest, I was bloody nervous. Boy oh boy, I'm telling you . . . When she lead me upstairs to her room, pulled the screen shut and there we were with the mattress on the floor! . . . But lo and behold. No Problems.

(Leaving his table and manuscript and sitting next to Donkeyman on the hatch. He nudges him in the

ribs) Last night Niigata . . . jig-jig three time. *(Relishing his memories)* Tiger now ready for Fiji sister. *(Pause. Tiger finally realizes he is getting no response from Donkeyman)* Hey! What's the matter? Why Donkeyman so glum? Little brother making jokes for big brother.

DONKEYMAN *(After a moment's thought)*: Why you no write, Tiger?

TIGER: What do you mean?

DONKEYMAN *(Refers to the manuscript)*: Tiger no write no more. Just talk this, talk that, but no andika.

TIGER *(Defensive)*: Oh, I see. Its like that is it. Time to get serious. Well . . . what do you think I'm going to do. Look—pen, ink, paper. Okay? Tiger write now. This isn't homework you know. It's a creative process and I must do it at my own inner rhythm. So just . . . stop staring and let me get on with it. *(Repositions his chair so that he has his back to Donkeyman. Another attempt to write but again nothing happens. Abandons his pen with a crooked little laugh)* It's perfect isn't it. The fucking Doldrums. Waveless and windless. Becalmed! The rotten old ship and the stupid bloody novel. *(Turns around to face Donkeyman)* Okay. So you want to know, why me no write?

DONKEYMAN: Sawa. Saba day now we leave u Japani, but same paypah. Tiger write nothing.

TIGER: Quite right. Seven days. I've also been counting. And if you want to be really exact its page one hundred and seventy-five that I've been staring at for seven days. Yes! Tiger no andika anymore. But why? *(Helpless gesture)* Me no know. You see me try. Tiger sit. Tiger dip him peni ya wino. Tiger wait . . . Nothing come! No feeling here *(His heart)*, no idea here *(His head)* Betty's done it. She's gone. Tiger try all time but no good. Nothing come. Maybe I'm burnt out. Or maybe I am just not a writer. Could be. And if it is . . . then what?

What am I? What the hell do I do with myself? Why am I here? . . . In the middle of bloody nowhere talking to somebody who doesn't understand a word of what I am saying. Oh, for God's sake, Donkeyman. Stop looking at me like that. If it means so much to you, go write your own bloody novel! *(Holding out his pen)* Here . . . you dip him, you write. *(Donkeyman gets up and leaves)* Oh shit. Now I've done it. *(Calling out)* I'm sorry!

SCENE 14

TIGER:

Dear Mom,

We've arrived in Fiji. We're anchored in a lagoon somewhere and we'll be here for a couple of very boring days—nobody is being allowed ashore for health reasons and we can't even swim next to the ship because the lagoon is full of sharks.

I'm feeling rather low at the moment, Mom. I'm homesick for good old P.E., and you and everybody else. And to make matters worse, my writing is not going so well at the moment. In fact, it is not going at all. I haven't added a word since Japan and I'm now beginning to feel really desperate. I think this is my first experience of what is called writer's block. You know you've got it somewhere inside you but you just can't find it and get it out and put it down on paper. I've got to do something, find something that will act as a release mechanism and open the flood gates once again. And you know how the saying goes, Mom: Where there's a will there's a way . . .

SCENE 15

Number four hatch. Tiger, under the influence of alcohol, humming a Franz Lehár melody, is waltzing around. He will get still more drunk as the scene progresses. Donkeyman appears on deck, watches Tiger for a few seconds, then settles down in his usual place and starts mending a garment with needle and cotton.

DONKEYMAN: Tiger happy happy.

TIGER: That, my dearly beloved big brother, is putting it mildly. Tiger plenty happy happy. Look *(The number at the top of a page)* . . . two hundred and three! You know what that means? Twenty-eight new pages! Twenty-eight damned good new pages. Yep. The floodgates have opened. I've had a breakthrough.

DONKEYMAN *(Sniffs the air, then goes to the table and smells the contents of Tiger's mug)*: Wiskey.

TIGER *(Finger to his lips and a wink)*: Ssssh! *(Looks around, then whispers)* I "borrowed" a bottle from the old man's stock. Want a swig?

DONKEYMAN *(Shaking his head)*: Ni si sawa, Tiger.

TIGER *(Wagging a finger)*: Now now—no bourgeois moralizing please, Mr. Donkeyman. It was for the sake of my art. I fuck for my art, I drink for my art, I live for my art. Relax, big brother, its only lubrication . . . and it works . . . the wheels are turning, turning . . . Betty has come back, and what's more, I'm taking her dancing. *(Sip from the mug)*

Here's the picture: Betty's got a new friend, Miranda Ferreira. She's a new waitress at the café and she has persuaded a very reluctant Betty to go with her to a dance. It's quite a posh affair in the Feather Market Hall, which of course makes Betty nervous. She's never been to a dance like that—she hasn't got a proper evening dress, and anyway she would rather just stay in her room and read and listen to the music of the young man playing the piano in the Palmerston Hotel, but Miranda is insistent. And she lends Betty an evening dress. *(He refers to his manuscript)* We're in her little room above the café. *(Reading)* "Betty pinned the little corsage of flowers over a firm young breast, then stood in front of the long wardrobe mirror, meaning to cast a severely critical eye over what she saw. Instead, she found herself blushing with pleasure and surprise. The transformation was startling. Gone was the awkward country girl of a year ago who had tramped the city streets in down-at-heel shoes looking for work.

"Staring back at her now with bright, eager eyes was a beautiful young woman ripe for a romantic adventure."

(Betty appears. She is as he describes. In the background, softly, a tango, played by Albert Sandler's Palm Court Orchestra.)

"The last items in her toilet were a light touch with a powder puff to each cheek and a little dab of English lavender on her wrists, after which she went back to the mirror for a final appraisal and then, quite involuntarily, she did something that made her heart skip a beat—she winked at herself! With a reckless little laugh she left her room and hurried down the stairs to the motorcar hooting impatiently in the street outside."

(He puts down his mug and manuscript and goes over to Betty, his open arms an invitation to dance.)

BETTY: I thought you would never ask. *(They laugh, they dance. Tiger, leading with authority, takes Betty through a little flourish in the dance)* I see you have learnt how to handle a woman.

TIGER: Do you approve?

BETTY: Oh, yes.

TIGER: So has your trust in me been restored?

BETTY: To tell you the truth, I never lost it.

TIGER: Then why have you been avoiding me?

BETTY: *Me* avoiding *you?* It's the other way around. I've been waiting very patiently for your summons. I thought it was you who had lost interest in me. I was even beginning to wonder if I would ever see you again.

TIGER: Whatever gave you that silly idea?

BETTY: Japan. Your "Niigata Nights."

TIGER: It was your doing. You chased me into her arms.

BETTY: But I didn't know you were going to *stay* there.

TIGER: Do I detect a note of jealousy?

BETTY: Of course. After all, I'm only a woman.

TIGER: You have nothing to worry about. That was just a passing amour. You know what they say about us seafarers—a girl in every port!

(They laugh, they dance.)

BETTY: And about you authors—a girl in every book.

TIGER: Ah, but do you want to know something, Betty? A different author, a different book, and you could steal Vronsky away from Madame Karenina tonight.

BETTY: Then why am I waltzing around here in limbo by myself? Please get on with it.

TIGER: Patience my dear. Patience. Don't let's go charging into something we are going to have to tear up later. This is a pivotal scene.

BETTY: Another one? Every time I'm ready to enjoy myself it becomes a pivotal scene. Can't I just have a plain, ordinary, good time for a change?

TIGER: You will. But in order to do that we must give it all the buildup we can. Explore those conflicting thoughts and feelings inside you.

BETTY *(Stamping her foot)*: No. I don't need anymore buildup. And I haven't got any conflicting thoughts and feelings. I just want to be happy. Now! I'm dressed and ready for it.

TIGER: Right. No arguments. We'll kick in with that. An impatient Betty.

BETTY: Oh yes!

TIGER: Feverishly impatient.

BETTY: . . . For whatever is going to happen to me tonight. Because I've got a feeling, a very simple, uncomplicated, no-conflicts feeling that something marvelous is going to happen to me tonight.

TIGER: Perfect. Here's the scenario. You arrive at the hall. Maybe there's a moment of hesitation outside—you're intimidated by all the smartly dressed people with their la-di-da voices and loud laughter. There's an impulse to turn around and run back to the safety of your little room, but you resist it. *(Quoting the text he will write)* "Hiding her turbulent feelings behind a mask of composure and self-possession, Betty stepped boldly into the bright lights of the Feather Market Hall. Flaunting her beauty with assurance and poise, she gaily abandoned herself to the evening's adventure. Her smooth white shoulders and slender neck gleamed like polished alabaster as she floated around the dance floor. Every Paul Jones ended in a small skirmish as the men, young and old, jostled each other to partner her in the next dance. Time passed unnoticed in this giddy whirl of waltzes and tangos, quicksteps and foxtrots."

BETTY *(Ecstatically happy)*: Yes! Yes! Go on. Keep it up.

TIGER: "But as the clock moved nearer the witching hour when the dance would end and everyone go home, a little voice inside Betty began to ask: Is this it? Is this all?"

Is this the happiness you so desperately wanted, Betty Le Roux . . . dancing with a different man each time?

These thoughts eat away like evil little worms at the golden apple of your expectations. You stop dancing. You refuse all the men who invite you back onto the dance floor. Your disenchantment with the evening becomes an overwhelming urge to escape. You head for the door. You're almost there when the music starts up again. It is your favorite tune.

BETTY: "Ramona."

TIGER: Instinctively you turn and look at the band. Until now they have just been a blurred image as you waltzed around the floor, but now you see them properly for the first time . . . and . . . ? *(Trying to coax the next development out of her)* Come on.

BETTY: What?

TIGER: What do you see?

BETTY: The band . . . and they're playing "Ramona."

TIGER: Is that all?

BETTY: Yes.

TIGER: No, it isn't. Look again.

BETTY: I'm looking.

TIGER: The man at the piano for God's sake. The pianist.

BETTY *(Taking her cue)*: No! It can't be.

TIGER: Yes it is. It's him. He's been watching you all night and is now totally under the spell of your beauty. He stands up, leaves the piano and starts walking towards you.

BETTY: What's he going to do?

TIGER: He is going to ask you to dance!

BETTY *(Shaking her head)*: No.

TIGER: No? Why? What's wrong?

BETTY: He can't.

TIGER: Of course he can! Don't spoil the scene, Betty. You wanted real happiness, well here it comes, striding to you across the dance floor. This is where you finally meet.

BETTY: You don't understand.

TIGER: Yes I do. And you're just being difficult again. Just imagine the band goes on playing without him . . . and even if they do stop, so what? That might even be a good idea. The band stops playing, everybody looks around to see what's going on . . .

BETTY: No no no. You don't understand. Its got nothing to do with the band or anything like that. It's him. He can't come "striding to me across the dance floor" and he can't dance because he's a cripple.

(The music stops. It won't be heard again. Tiger is speechless for a few seconds.)

TIGER *(Confused)*: Where the hell does that come from? A cripple? *(Fumbling through his manuscript)* Did I say that? . . . No . . . Where . . . No . . . I didn't say he was a cripple.

BETTY: I said it.

TIGER: Why?

BETTY: Because I know. I saw it.

One night in my room there above the café, I was lying on my bed as usual waiting for him to start playing, but when he did I could almost not hear it. It sounded far away. I went to my window and looked out. They had closed the big hotel lounge window and drawn the curtains. I suddenly felt very desperate. His music was the only beautiful thing I had in my life. I couldn't carry on without it. I had to hear him, I had to see him. So I plucked up all my courage and put on my best dress and went around to the hotel. I was very nervous. I had never been in a place like that before. I ordered a cooldrink from the waiter and sat down in a corner and pretended I was waiting for somebody. And there he was, at the other end of the room. I enjoyed just watching him almost as much as I did listening to his music. Everything about him was so gentle and careful—like the way he would turn the pages of a music album, one at a time, until he found the tune he was looking for, and then start playing. Or the way he drank the beer which a customer had sent him, always wiping his mouth afterwards . . .

TIGER: . . . with a neatly folded, white handkerchief!

BETTY: That's right. When I saw that I knew he was a gentleman.

TIGER: A perfect gentleman. To the manner born. "Please" and "thank you," "excuse me" and "pardon me" and of course . . . *(Doffing an imaginary hat)* "A good day to you, madam." I never heard him use bad language once. Even when he was drunk, I never heard a single swearword come from his lips. And not a single act of violence. He never once raised a hand to me or my mother. Not even so much as a threat.

BETTY *(Nodding agreement)*: I could see it in his face, in his quiet smile and gentle blue eyes.

TIGER *(Pained pride)*: That's him. That's my father.

BETTY: I could have sat there all night listening to him, but when the city hall clock started to strike ten he stopped playing. We all clapped and he half-turned on the piano stool and gave a little bow. He put away his music and carefully closed the piano. Then I saw the crutches, because he reached over to one side for them. They were leaning against the wall. I hadn't noticed them before. He stood up, put one under each arm and started to leave. He had to pass the table where I was sitting and I thought he wasn't going to see me because he had his eyes fixed on the ground in front of him. But at the very last moment he lifted his head, looked into my eyes and smiled.

TIGER: Yep. Very good. That is exactly how my mother tells it.

(He drifts away from Betty and lands up next to Donkeyman.)

The old girl wasn't exaggerating. Boy, was he good looking. A little bit like Tyrone Power you know. There's a picture of him as a young man with his band—The Melodians—and I'm telling you, I don't blame my mom. He was a charmer all right. And what's more, he came from one of Port Elizabeth's best English-speaking families. Sounds perfect doesn't it. My mom couldn't have asked for more. And she didn't . . . and that was a big mistake. But it's not going to happen again. He's my father and I love him, but . . . No! Not in here . . . *(He indicates his manuscript)*

(He returns to Betty) No! You can't have him!

BETTY: Why not?

TIGER: Because he's not in here. *(The manuscript in his hands)* That's why not. This is your life and nowhere in here does it say or will it ever say anything about a cripple or crutches. He doesn't exist for you. Use your imagination for God's sake! A cripple on the dance floor? Is that what you want? People laughing and staring while you try waltzing around with a pair of crutches?

BETTY: Are you ashamed of your father?

TIGER: No!

BETTY: Then why are you denying him?

TIGER: I'm not! . . . I'm just . . . Am I really? . . . No! No, I am not denying him. I'm denying nothing. I just don't want you to make the same mistake. *(His manuscript)* Because don't think he's going to be sitting there in the Palmerston Hotel lounge for the rest of his life looking handsome and earning a few bob a week playing "Ramona." He's going to start drinking and hitting the wrong notes and you are going to end up sacrificing every dram you've got to feed and clothe three bawling kids and a useless cripple. Your dreams don't stand a chance if you go with him.

BETTY: It's too late. I love him.

TIGER *(A little laugh of despair and defeat)*: Bravo! You've done it again. That was my mom talking all right. So go on . . . you know what comes next . . . *(He sings)*

Oh sweet mystery of life at last I've found you,
For its love and love alone . . .

Her all-time favorite song. She always remembers how in the early years, she used to stand at the piano and sing it while he played. Pretty picture, isn't it. The two of them young and in love. You want a picture of them now, Betty Le Roux? *(Struggling to control a befuddled thought process so as to be as accurate as possible)* She's . . . sitting on the side of her bed . . . her tired old nightie clammy with sweat—the sweat of desperation . . . clutching her asthma spray with one hand, scratching her graying head with the other. She's trying to work out how she can make the few quid she's got in her bag, pay the café rent, and the boys' wages, and the baker, and the cooldrink man, and the Cadbury's man and all the other bloody parasites that feed off her life. She goes over that pathetic little bit of mental arithmetic again and again, but it never works out . . . She hasn't got enough . . . She'll never have enough. Her once beautiful, brown eyes are little pools of anxiety and fear. He is lying in his bed, a few feet away from her, reading old comic books with a magnifying glass . . . *Superman, Batman, Submariner*—WHAM! BAM! POW! CRASH! KAZOOM!—with a magnifying glass. Those wonderful, blue eyes are still unclouded . . . his fine aristocratic features and complexion smooth and unlined . . . They have the repose of a death mask. He stopped playing the piano a long time ago and she doesn't dream any-more.

Crazy isn't it? I thought I could escape all that . . . be free. And it looks as if I have, doesn't it? I mean, here I am—Fiji for God's sake, the beautiful and romantic South Pacific, moonlight shimmering on a palm-fringed lagoon, thousands of miles away from that shabby little world that spawned me. But you want to know some-thing? I'm not really here—I'm back there. Yep! This isn't real—this balmy tropical night, that moon, this ship, this lagoon full of sharks. God, I wish it was . . . that I could claim it as mine. This is my World and I am Free! I can't. I belong to that room, to that world of silent music and dead dreams. And so do you.

(Pause.)

It's time for us to go back, Betty. Yep. There's no escape . . . for me or for you. *(His manuscript)* I thought I could at least give you one on paper, but even that won't work. I can't make a happy ending out of my dad.

(He throws the manuscript overboard and then goes and sits at his table. Betty and Donkeyman go to the ship's rail and look over the side.)

BETTY: The ink is already running, the words starting to blur and drift off the pages. It's like bleeding to death . . . after all, it was my life. I can feel it ebbing away. A few more seconds and there won't be a word of it left.

DONKEYMAN *(Turning to Tiger)*: Why you do that? *(Tiger, mute with misery, lifts shoulders and hands in a help-less gesture)* No! Lazima uangee, Tiger. You must speak, Tiger. Why? Ni uango pia—it is also for me! Ndiyo!

BETTY *(To Tiger)*: A real writer wouldn't have worried about happy endings, you know. He would let the cripples go onto the dance floor and live with the consequences.

(She disappears.)

DONKEYMAN: You throw paypah into sea but is also for Donkeyman. Long time you na me we sit every night an you write—Port Sudan, Port Aden, Colombo, Singapore, Niigata, Fiji. Me na you. Donkeyman na Tiger. Rafiki. Ndugu mdogo na ndugu mkubwa. Big brother, little brother. You tell me is good you write—Donkeyman give cigarette. You tell me is more good—Donkeyman give beer, Donkeyman pay jig-jig. Now you throw paypah in sea. Why? Umeni saleti, umevunja urafiki yetu! You no speak Tiger?

(Tiger remains mute. In a sudden and savage action Donkeyman reduces the garment he was mending to shreds and throws the pieces to one side. He goes to the table, takes Tiger's open fountain pen and dips it carefully in the ink bottle, wiping the nib on the side of the bottle as he has seen Tiger do a hundred times, and then puts it in Tiger's hand.)

You write . . . Bullshit!

(He leaves.)

SCENE 16

AUTHOR: A few days later our sailing orders came through on the radio: proceed with cargo to the Port of Greenock in the Firth of Clyde. After the last bag of sugar was loaded and the hatches battened down, we upped anchor and set off on our long haul to Scotland. Back in Port Elizabeth, my dad dutifully got out his map, red pencil and ruler and started to draw straight lines across the Pacific—Fiji to Honolulu, Honolulu to San Pedro, then Balboa and the Panama Canal, and finally all the way up the Atlantic to the British Isles. It was the end of my big adventure. I knew I was going home. As for Donkeyman . . . he never spoke to me again after that night. Never so much as even acknowledged my existence. I had thrown a lot more than just my manuscript overboard.

But that wasn't really the end of him. I wouldn't go so far as to say he haunts me, but sometimes when I'm working I get a quiet feeling that I'm being watched, that someone is sitting there watching me while I write. And just occasionally, when it's been a really good session, suddenly there's a tin of fifty Woodbine cigarettes there on the table in front of me. I light one, sit back and take a deep drag . . . and hear Donkeyman laugh again. He reminds me that I and my writing belong to a world where a lot of people can't put words on paper and tell their stories. And then of course, there's Betty. All in white, remember everything white!—Hat, dress, gloves, shoes and stockings, a little necklace of beads around her throat, and at her waist a little red rosebud . . .

(Betty appears. She is the shy, demure young woman we first met.)

BETTY: Please tell my story.
AUTHOR: Oh Betty, are you never going to give up?
BETTY: No. Please! That's all I want.
AUTHOR: That's all you want? You don't think that's a lot?
BETTY: Is it?
AUTHOR: Yes it is. You're asking for a life.

BETTY: Because you promised me one . . . a long time ago remember . . . and you haven't kept that promise.

AUTHOR: I know.

BETTY: So then don't you owe it to me to try just once more. Please! I really will behave myself this time. I'll do everything you want me to. No arguments. And it will be so much easier for you now. You're so much more experienced. You'll know how to handle me. Is that really asking for such a lot?

AUTHOR: More than a lot—you're asking for the impossible.

BETTY: No I'm not. Look at all the other stories you've already told.

AUTHOR: Acts of contrition, Betty.

BETTY: What do you mean?

AUTHOR: When I aborted your story that night in Fiji, I was left with the feeling that I had committed a terrible sin. It already had a heartbeat you see, a life of its own . . . and I threw it to the sharks! All the others I've told since then . . . attempts at penance.

BETTY: So then haven't you had enough of all that now? You're old you know. Aren't you tired? Don't you want to make my story your last one? Your first failure, your last great success . . . then you will be able to rest in peace.

AUTHOR: My last story?

BETTY: Yes!

AUTHOR: No! Those are terrible words. They frighten me! If I knew I only had one story left to tell I'd be too frightened to tell it. I'd feel like a condemned man who had reached his last day.

BETTY: Well I'm not going to give up on you know.

AUTHOR: Please don't! You've become my muse, Betty. Your visits keep me going. But come, its the end of the watch. Do you want to strike it?

BETTY: All right. How many times?

AUTHOR: Eight.

(Betty strikes eight bells.)

BETTY: As simple as that?
AUTHOR: As simple as that.

(They leave the stage together.)

END OF PLAY

GLOSSARY

ANDIKA	To write
EEBWANA UNA SEEMA NI NI EN DE LEAH	What are you saying?
FAHAMU	Understand
KIJANA	Young woman
KUBWA	Variation of "proud"
KWAHERI	Good-bye
LALA SALAMA	Good night
LAZIMA UANGEE	Talk to me
MKONO	Hand
MUHIMU	Variation of "proud"
MZURI	Okay
NASHAKURU	Thank you
NDIYO	Yes
NDUGU MDOGO NA NDUGU MKUBWA	Big brother and little brother
NI UANGO PIA	It is also mine
NINI HII	What is it?
PENI YA WINO	Fountain pen
RAFIKI	Friend
SANA	Very much

GLOSSARY

SAWA	Okay
SIKILIZA	To listen
SOMA	To read
TUTAONANA BAADAYE	See you later
UTANDO WAMADATISO	Is difficult

ATHOL FUGARD has been working in the theatre as a playwright, director and actor since the 1950s. His plays have been produced throughout his native South Africa, as well as in major theatres across the United States and abroad. His previous works include *Blood Knot, Boesman and Lena, Cousins: A Memoir, Hello and Goodbye, A Lesson from Aloes, Marigolds in August, The Guest, "Master Harold" . . . and the boys, My Children! My Africa!, Notebooks: 1960–1977, Playland, A Place with the Pigs, The Road to Mecca, Statements* and *Valley Song.*